Original title:
Life's Lessons: Brought to You by Puns

Copyright © 2025 Creative Arts Management OÜ
All rights reserved.

Author: Elliot Harrison
ISBN HARDBACK: 978-1-80566-149-8
ISBN PAPERBACK: 978-1-80566-444-4

Jest in Time

A clock once told a joke, so fine,
But it ticked away, lost in its time.
To laugh is to live, or so they say,
Just watch that old clock, don't let it sway.

A pun can make the grumpiest cheer,
Like a cat in a hat, just spreading good cheer.
When words play tricks, the fun begins,
As smiles abound, it's where laughter wins.

Blunders Become Wonders

A baker's dough rose, claiming its fame,
But burnt like my toast—oh, what a shame!
Mistakes in the kitchen, a humorous feast,
Causing giggles, at least, to say the least.

A child's spilled juice, a colorful mess,
Like abstract art—who knew of this stress?
With every faux pas, a lesson is spun,
In laughter we find, life's more fun!

Pun Intended: The Growth of Humor

Weed 'n' seeds grow where laughter does bloom,
A garden of jokes clears away the gloom.
With every punchline, we nurture the plot,
In humor we find, it's all we've got.

From flowers to fruits, puns harvest delight,
Each giggle a seed, planted just right.
As we water these quips, they flourish and thrive,
Through jest, we discover—we're joyfully alive.

Insightful Irony

A fish in a tree dreams of deep seas,
While a bird in the water aims to just breeze.
Irony abounds in the quirkiest tales,
Where life's like a ship, with unpredictable sails.

Sometimes we trip on the jokes that we share,
Yet laughter is sprinkled through trials we bear.
In irony's grip, we find clever little clues,
Like a pun in the dark, to light up our views.

Fun on the Run

Jogging through life with a smile in tow,
Puns take the lead, oh how they flow.
Speed bumps of laughter, I trip and I fall,
But with each silly slip, I stand up tall.

Skipping on paths, where jokes grow wild,
Like a child with candy, so playfully styled.
Running in circles, but still on the chase,
In this race of puns, there's no time to waste.

Puns of the Heart.

My heart races fast, it's a pun-derful game,
Each beat's a chuckle, never quite the same.
When love comes knocking, it takes a good shot,
With words so cheesy, it's a spicy hot knot.

Cupids with quips, shoot arrows so bright,
In this pun-laden romance, everything's light.
Every sweet whisper, a wordplay delight,
Together we laugh, from morning to night.

The Wisdom of Witty Words

In the garden of humor, thoughts start to bloom,
Witty words grow tall, dispelling the gloom.
Plant seeds of laughter, watch joy intertwine,
For wisdom in jest, is simply divine.

Rusty old sayings get polished with glee,
Turning dull moments to comedy spree.
For every lesson learned, there's a punchline near,
With puns as our compass, we navigate cheer.

Pun Intended: A Journey Through Humor

Embarking on journeys where laughter is key,
Navigating woes with a pun-filled decree.
Each step is a giggle, a twist in the plot,
Inventive wordplay heats up every thought.

Road signs of humor mark paths that we tread,
With laughter as fuel, we're happily led.
So buckle up tight for this whimsical ride,
For humor's our guide, and puns are our pride.

Punning the Past

When I was young, I had a ball,
But now it seems I dropped it all.
Time flies by, it's hard to catch,
Just like my hopes—oh what a mismatch!

My past's a pun, a joke on me,
A twist of fate, can't you see?
Lessons learned, oh what a blast,
I laugh at shadows of the past!

Rhyme and Reason

Why did the tomato turn so red?
Because it saw the salad dress instead!
A rhyme in life is often missed,
A slip of wit that can't be kissed.

The punchlines come, they waltz and tease,
Life cracks up like a ball of cheese.
With every chuckle, wisdom flows,
A world of giggles, this one knows!

The Folly of Forgetfulness

I lost my keys, but found a pen,
A trade of wit I'd do again.
Forget my phone? Oh that's just grand,
But I remember where to stand!

Thus folly strikes, what a fine art,
For getting jokes is where we start.
Forget the past, but not the fun,
We laugh together, you and I, as one!

Wit Meets Wisdom

Why did the wise man cross the street?
To teach the chicken, life's a treat!
Wit and wisdom play their game,
And give a chuckle, not the same.

As wisdom grows, the jokes will sprout,
In every laugh, there's truth no doubt.
So raise a glass, let friendships bloom,
With puns and laughs, we fill the room!

The Joy of Just Kidding: A Thoughtful Ponder

A joke too close to home can sting,
But laughter's the best gift we bring.
When things go wrong, just take a pause,
With a chuckle, you'll find your cause.

A pun a day keeps gloom away,
It brightens up the dullest day.
So roll with the winks and silly jibes,
They'll stitch together all the vibes.

When life gives you lemons, make a spritz,
And serve them with some playful wits.
When troubles bubble up like gum,
A giggle's the best way to overcome.

So here's to wit that lifts our soul,
Pun after pun, we reach our goal.
In every jest, a treasure hides,
Let joy be where your heart abides.

Laugh Lines: The Path of Experience

Through the ups and downs we weave,
Each comic twist is hard to believe.
With every slip and silly fall,
A hearty laugh can conquer all.

Seasoned with humor, life's a treat,
Like shoes that pinch, but still look neat.
Embrace the quirks, the slapstick flair,
For in the chaos, joy is rare.

Like garlic bread that warms the heart,
A pun can play a vital part.
With friends around, we find our song,
In mirthful moments, we all belong.

So laugh with me, let humor fly,
For life's too short to question why.
Each laugh line tells a story sweet,
In every jest, our lives complete.

A Canopy of Comedy: Shades of Insight

Underneath the laughter's shade,
With every pun, a bridge is laid.
Tickle your ribs and take a seat,
In humor's world, we find our feet.

When life becomes a circus show,
A punster's wink will help you grow.
So take a bow, embrace the jest,
In fun-filled chaos, we feel blessed.

A wisecrack here, a giggle there,
With laughter's grace, we take our share.
For silly moments mean the most,
In levity, we love to boast.

With friends who laugh, the sun will shine,
In comical tales, our hearts align.
So sip that punch, enjoy the ride,
For in this jest, we all collide.

The Nuance of Nonsense

Nonsense reigns where fun begins,
It spins the world on cheeky grins.
When things get serious, hold your bay,
And let the puns lead you astray.

Wit sprinkled top like sugar on cake,
Brings levity to every mistake.
A laugh that rolls, a rhyme that sings,
Just watch how joy transforms all things.

Life's a pun with twists and turns,
In witty ways, the wisdom churns.
So gather 'round, don't take a pause,
In nonsense, we find our applause.

Here's to the quirks that make us whole,
With laughter sweet for every soul.
In playful chaos, wisdom blooms,
With every chuckle, joy resumes.

Humorous Echoes of Experience

In the garden of fate, weeds grow tall,
Laughter's what we need, to not trip and fall.
When the pie's in the sky, it's hard to complain,
A slice of humor makes the frame less plain.

If you find life a joke, try not to frown,
Just remember, the punchline won't let you down.
Like a pun in the wind, it may take you by surprise,
A chuckle can spring from the silliest guise.

The Punchline of Growth

Why did the scarecrow win an award?
Because he was outstanding in his field, adored.
In the classroom of time, the jesters hold sway,
Life's riddles unveil a smile each day.

When the road gets tough, just take a detour,
Sometimes the random path can lead to more.
Each stumble, a chance to trip with finesse,
Turns a serious stumble into humorous mess.

Laughing at Lessons: A Punny Perspective

Why don't scientists trust atoms anymore?
Because they make up everything, that's folklore.
In life's grand theater, joy steals the show,
With puns as the script, watch the laughter grow.

Every slip and fall, a tickle to the soul,
Funny how it warms the angst, makes us whole.
Lessons weave through laughter's delightful embrace,
It seems comical wisdom's the ultimate grace.

The Lighthearted Truth

Why did the bicycle fall over and weep?
It was two-tired to pedal, lost in the deep.
Like a jester at court, truth wears a grin,
In the light of the jest, let the fun begin.

When life gives you puzzles, solve them with flair,
Add a sprinkle of laughs, creativity in the air.
Each quirk that we mirror, those puns that we send,
Are the treasures in laughs that teach us to mend.

Pundamental Truths

In a world where jokes can sting,
Be careful which puns you bring.
Tie up your laughter with a bow,
For wit blooms best when puns can grow.

Don't trust a math pun, they're known to divide,
Keep your humor close, let it be your guide.
In every riddle, there's hidden delight,
Just turn it around, and it's better in sight.

A fish without puns is just a catch,
Next time you're fishing, make it a match.
Wit is the hook, laughter a reel,
For every punchline, there's joy to steal.

So gather your jokes, let them unfurl,
A life that laughs can really twirl.
In the garden of wit, may you bloom bright,
With puns in your pocket, you'll conquer the night.

The Jest in the Journey

On the road of humor, twist and shout,
Every pun you take's a detour route.
With laughter as fuel, let's not forget,
The more you chuckle, the less you fret.

As we cruise through the valleys of jest,
Remember, puns always pass the test.
From corny fries to jokes in a stew,
Each laugh we share helps lighten the view.

When life gives you lemons, make a pun,
Squeeze the best out, don't leave any fun.
For each twist and turn will teach you well,
In laughter's embrace, there's a magic spell.

So pack in the giggles, fill your cup,
With laughter and joy, let's all lift up.
Through jest and humor, our spirits will soar,
For each funny moment opens a door.

Puns and Roses: The Thorns of Growth

A garden grows best with laughs and dreams,
Where puns sprout up like sunbeams.
Watch out for thorns that poke and tease,
In humor's embrace, find joy and ease.

Plant a seed of wit, give it time,
Soon blossoms of laughter will begin to climb.
Even weeds can tickle your sides,
When you see them as puns in disguise.

When petals fall, don't take offense,
Just turn them into a funny pretense.
For every rose has its prickly part,
And laughter softens even the hardest heart.

So nurture your garden with puns galore,
Let humor bloom, and watch it soar.
In the landscape of jest, you'll always find,
A patch of joy that's wonderfully kind.

Chuckles in the Classroom

In the classroom of life, don't keep a straight face,
For humor's the teacher that teaches with grace.
When lessons go wrong, just giggle and jest,
A pun in your pocket will help with the test.

Math might be tough, but humor adds flair,
Imagine your numbers as dancing in air.
History's tales can be given a twist,
With puns as your guide, you can't be missed.

Science experiments often go boom,
So sprinkle in laughs to lighten the gloom.
With giggles in goggles, you'll conquer the task,
Each chuckle a lesson, just dare to ask!

In this school of jest, make laughter your art,
For every good pun is a friend to the heart.
So gather around, let's learn and play,
In this chuckling classroom, we'll seize the day!

Giggles and Grit: Wisdom Wrapped in Humor

A baker's dozen teaches me,
To rise, just knead, and see.
If life hands dough, don't pout,
Make a pizza and stretch it out!

Embrace the puns, they never quit,
Even when we sometimes sit.
To taco 'bout it, don't forget,
Lettuce laugh, no need for fret!

In seas of troubles, just float by,
Don't dive deep, just surf the high.
Whale you may, swim with a grin,
Catch the waves, let the fun begin!

So when in doubt, just pun away,
Wear a smile, come what may.
For every twist, a joke will key
To life's great dance; it sets you free!

The Quirk of Existence: Puns as Narratives

Why did the grape stop in place?
It ran out of juice in the race!
Life's always a punny spree,
Jokes and laughs, just wait and see.

Comparing ducks to the quack,
Adventure calls; there's no lack.
Follow the breadcrumbs laid in fun,
Every pun's a shine of the sun!

A slice of cheese? Don't take it hard,
Just relish the moments; it's not a card.
The dairy puns may seem quite gouda,
But with laughter, they become a sudra!

Tell me what's cheesy? A silly grin,
For every fail, that's where you win.
In jest and jive, learn to aspire,
To dance with puns, let your soul inspire!

Sage Jests: Wisdom Behind the Laughter

Knock-knock jokes open the door,
To wisdom wrapped in laughter's lore.
Is there a pun with sentiment?
Yes, if you just give it a bent!

What do you call a fake noodle?
An impasta, the jester's poodle.
In life's wild chase, don't go straight,
A twist of humor can navigate!

Be cautious with puns, they can sprout,
Laughing can lead to joy throughout.
But don't let laughter turn to jest,
For wise cracks don't always rest!

So take a breath and with a cheer,
Share a pun that's crystal clear.
In every giggle, let it sink,
There's wisdom hidden in the wink!

The Smart Side of Silly

A circus of laughs fills the air,
Jokes on every corner, flair to spare.
Why did the clown cross the street?
To make the funny dance complete!

Giggle like a toddler with a toy,
Remembering age, oh what a ploy!
For each burst of laughter, a lesson too,
Silly antics, they guide us through.

A frog's ribbit echoes a tale,
In lily pads where giggles prevail.
Hopping to punchlines, find your beat,
In puns, my friend, life's a treat!

Each joke's a doorway, wide and bright,
To wisdom seen through laughter's light.
When in doubt, play the fool,
For in silly jest, we make the rules!

The Gag That Teaches

A pun can save the day, they say,
When humor leads the way,
When jokes are dressed in wisdom's cloak,
You learn the art with each fun poke.

A fishy tale can teach you well,
If you catch the scent, you can tell,
In every jest, there lies a clue,
A lesson learned with laughter too.

Tickle your brain with puns so bright,
Illuminate the dark of night,
For every quip, a laugh will flow,
And in that joy, the truth will grow.

So don't just laugh, embrace the jest,
In puns, we find what we're blessed,
The gag that teaches lights the way,
To wisdom wrapped in humor's play.

Laugh LIKE A Lesson: Pun-driven Insights

When the lights go out, don't fear the dark,
A lovely pun will leave a mark,
To toast the bread, you must let it rest,
And from each pun, you'll find the best.

Why did the tomato turn so red?
Because it saw the salad spread!
In every joke, there's wisdom ripe,
Harvesting humor, it's your type.

With shoes untied, you trip and fall,
But laughter helps you stand up tall,
In each misstep, there's joy to greet,
The lesson learned with rhythm and beat.

So laugh like a lesson, learn like a kid,
Embrace the puns, don't let them hid,
For every chuckle brings delight,
Wisdom dances in the light.

Roars of Realization: Discovery Through Humor

A bear walks in and steals the show,
With one good pun, he steals your woe,
As laughter echoes through the trees,
Realization kicks with playful ease.

In jokes, we find a clever thread,
To weave our thoughts, brilliant and spread,
Through roars of giggles and grins so wide,
Discovery blooms when punchlines collide.

A snail once said, without a frown,
Why rush when you can take your crown?
Finding joy in every slow,
Is how true wisdom tends to grow.

So listen close to humor's call,
In laughter's grip, we rise or fall,
With roars of fun come insights bright,
A clever jest brings truth to light.

Mirthful Musings: The Inspiration of Puns

In every chuckle, there's a seed,
For growth and joy, it's all you need,
With puns to plant, your heart will burst,
The sweetest laughter quenches thirst.

A cactus can't hug, but don't despair,
For prickly times are a joke to share,
In mirthful musings, we thrive and sway,
The lessons bloom in playful array.

Wise owls hoot with wisdom's dance,
Their puns invite you to take a chance,
So ponder well these joyful sounds,
In witty twists, true wisdom abounds.

Let laughter guide your wandering heart,
In every jest, you'll play your part,
With mirthful musings, ideas arise,
Puns light the way, the clever prize.

Laughing Matters: The Serious Side of Jokes

A pun walked into a bar, took a seat,
"I'm here for a laugh, isn't that neat?"
The bartender grinned, pouring him some cheer,
"Just remember, my friend, punchlines are near!"

A riddle strolled by, wearing a grin,
"Why did the chicken? Let's begin!"
Life's quirks can be fun, so embrace a jest,
In humor, some wisdom can truly manifest.

An anagram danced, jiving with glee,
"Listen closely now, can you see me?"
Letters can shift, create a new state,
Change your perspective, it might be great!

So gather round friends, let laughter unite,
In the face of troubles, keep humor in sight.
For even in jest, there's a truth to be found,
In laughter, the heaviest hearts can rebound.

Wordplay and Wisdom: A Reflection

Once a wise sage said, 'Words play and tease,'
Each twist in the tale brings us to our knees.
Why cry over spilled milk when there's cheese?
A grin can unite, spread joy with ease!

There's wisdom in jokes, disguised in plain sight,
A pun can open worlds, set hearts alight.
Like a koala's hug, a comfort to find,
Wrap yourself in laughter, it's genuinely kind!

A tongue twister whirled, spinning so fast,
"Fickle feasted friends, shadows they cast!"
But pause and reflect, let the meaning sink,
In playful chaos, link thoughts in a blink!

So let playful puns teach us and guide,
In the garden of humor, let joy reside.
For every chuckle, a lesson we share,
In the folly of life, there's room for good care.

Learning Through Laughter: A Poetic Guide

Once a joker decided to teach us some grace,
With jokes up his sleeve, he smiled with great face.
"What's orange and sounds like a parrot?" he cried,
"A carrot!" he roared, and giggles replied.

In life's funny moments, we often observe,
A twist or a pun can give us the verve.
So take a moment, when times get tough,
Remember those laughs — they're plenty enough!

A pun was perplexed, feeling a bit blue,
"I'm just clever words, but what's my real cue?"
But then came a lesson, crisp as a cucumber,
Humor can heal, like a thunderous number!

So gather your jokes, your laughter and cheer,
In playful exchange, it's the joy we endear.
From silly to serious, all things entwined,
In the laughter we share, true wisdom we find.

Puns of the Past: Echoes of Insight

In days of yore, where the jesters did play,
A pun on the past kept the worries at bay.
"Why don't scientists trust atoms?" they'd muse,
"Because they make up everything!" They'd choose.

With laughter as armor, we'd tackle each plot,
The echoes of humor, a brave, cozy lot.
A figure of speech, sharp as a dart,
Delivering wisdom straight to the heart!

From words that rhyme to those that surprise,
Puns weave through life, like sweet lullabies.
The path may be twisted; there's fun to be had,
In the game of the mind, it's never too bad!

So celebrate puns, those sly little tricks,
For laughter's a language that everyone picks.
With echoes of insight, let's share in the jest,
For a chuckle together is truly the best!

Puns as Pillars: Foundations of Insight

Words can twist and neatly bend,
A simple joke can be your friend.
A pun in hand is worth your time,
It lifts the mood and sparks the rhyme.

In every jest, a truth may shine,
Like grapes that tell a wine-filled line.
With puns we find our laughter's grace,
In irony, we find our place.

When life gives lemons, what a treat!
A lemonade that's bittersweet.
Don't take the world too seriously,
In every crack, there's comedy.

So when you stumble, trip, or fall,
Just laugh it off, you'll stand up tall.
For every mishap has a chance,
To turn a frown into a dance.

Laughing Lessons: The Hidden Teachings

A rooster's call starts off the show,
It's time to rise, don't be too slow.
For every pun that tickles ribs,
A lesson lies within the jibs.

The snail's slow crawl is quite a race,
In patience, we find our own pace.
From fishy tales to bear-y puns,
We learn from critters that weigh tons.

When clouds bring rain, just dance about,
For puddles form, there's no doubt.
In every drop, a splash of bliss,
In humor's grasp, we find our kiss.

So open wide, your heart to play,
Embrace the fun, come what may.
From chuckles found in every turn,
We find the wisdom we will learn.

The Irony of Insight: A Comedic Walk

A cat that purrs is also sly,
With feathered friends up in the sky.
When irony meets jest so grand,
We find the truth all unplanned.

A baker's dough may rise with glee,
While loafing 'round, it longs to be.
Each pun is baked at just the right heat,
To serve us wisdom we can eat.

In every joke, a kernel waits,
Like handing peanuts to the mates.
A humor's touch can set us free,
Through laughter's lens, we truly see.

So step with care on this funny path,
And take a moment for a laugh.
For in each pun, there lies a truth,
That dances lightly in our youth.

Chuckles and Change: A Poetic Dance

Life's like a dance, with steps so bold,
We twirl with humor, break the mold.
In rhythms of joy, we find our feet,
   With funny lines, we feel the beat.

Each giggle's spark ignites a flame,
To light the way through life's wild game.
Like bees with buzz, we learn to sting,
With puns and laughter, we found our wing.

So glide through troubles, skip the woe,
   For every fumble helps us grow.
In every chuckle, there's a chance,
   To turn our trials into dance.

Embrace the joy, let laughter ring,
For in this world, it's the greatest thing.
With puns and chuckles, we rearrange,
   Our lives become a playful change.

Witty Revelations: The Art of Insight

A pun in the hand's worth two in the bush,
Make folks chuckle with that clever push.
Wit dances lightly on the tongue,
While laughs and giggles keep us young.

Why did the scarecrow win a prize?
Because he was outstanding, oh what a surprise!
The cornier the jokes, the more we cheer,
We gather the puns and hold them dear.

Bakers always rise to the occasion,
Kneaded humor, the best persuasion.
Inserting a joke into a recipe,
Is like icing on cake, oh so heavenly!

So take a moment, lighten your load,
The road of humor is a joyous road.
With each clever word and hearty jest,
Laughter expands, humor's the best!

The Serious Side of Satire

If you can't take a joke, it's just a shame,
The punchlines hit harder than you might claim.
A satirist's pen, sharp as a knife,
Cuts through the layers of everyday life.

What's black, white, and read all over?
A newspaper, but it's not a great cover!
We flip the script for a dose of fun,
Turning mundane groans into laughter won.

Politicians' smiles, a sight to behold,
Their actions are tales that need to be told.
A jester's crown is wiser than gold,
With a pinch of irony, the truth unfolds.

So chuckle at the world and let it be bright,
In satire we see both wrong and right.
With every jest, we uncork the fizz,
Finding clarity in humor's quiz!

When Humor Hits Home

A pun a day keeps gloom at bay,
When life is tough, laugh anyway!
The cat next door thinks he's a king,
When he trips on air—oh, what a fling!

Why did the chicken cross the road?
To get to the fun or lose the load?
Each cluck's a reminder, don't take yourself too,
For even the fowl find humor in the blue.

In love and laughter, we learn to cope,
Knocking on life's door, we find the hope.
With jokes on the table, bring forth the cheer,
Family dinners filled with jeers!

So embrace the silly, the clear, the bright,
Let laughter echo into the night.
In the end, it's the smiles we spread,
That light the journey, where laughter's widespread!

Guffaws of Growth

Growing wiser doesn't mean we forget,
To joke and laugh, oh what a debt!
As we bloom like flowers in the sun's glare,
We swap out seriousness for good care.

What do you call fake spaghetti?
An impasta! A pun that's steady!
In every blunder, there's growth to find,
Through bursts of laughter, we clear the mind.

As we tumble and fall on this fun ride,
Let the world's quirks be our playful guide.
With every slip, we learn some grace,
Lifting each other in this silly race.

So take a step back, relax, and unwind,
In laughter we discover life's true kind.
For when giggles abound and spirits dance,
Every day offers a chance for a chance!

Quips and Queries: A Journey of Insight

In the great library of jest,
A book with no spine is the best.
The pages are blank, filled with dreams,
Yet wisdom unfurls in soft, silly beams.

Questions may wag their funny tails,
As laughter through knowledge prevails.
Why did the scarecrow win a prize?
He was outstanding in his field—what a surprise!

Each riddle unwrapped leads to a grin,
Like a fish caught trying to swim in a tin.
Inquiries prance on the tip of a lip,
The voyage of wit—come take a trip!

So gather your quirks and don't be shy,
There's humor found in the low hanging pie.
Dig deep in the jest, no need to fret,
For insight arrives sans a major vignette.

The Comedic Compass

With a compass of chuckles, I set my course,
Navigating through humor, a playful force.
Why did the chicken cross the sea?
To get to the other tide, just wait and see!

Jokes are the markers guiding my way,
Leading me forth to the light of the day.
I've got a friend who's a baker; it's true,
He kneads the dough—how about you?

Through valleys of puns, on laughter I tread,
With a wink and a smile, no need to be fed.
Each twist and each turn brings a brand-new jest,
In this comedy map, we all are guests.

Where laughter flows like a bubbling brook,
Amusing adventures in every nook.
So grab your giggles, and don't look back,
With a comedic compass, we're on the right track.

A Punning Pathway to Truth

Strolling down puns akin to wide lanes,
Where laughter's the ticket and joy reigns.
Why do seagulls fly over the ocean blue?
Because if they flew over the bay, they'd be bagels too!

Each chuckle a step on this curvy trail,
With puns as my guide, I'll never fail.
I met a gardener who's never late,
He's always on thyme, isn't that great?

With a trowel of wit and a plant full of cheer,
I dig deep for laughter, I hold it dear.
Life's complexities wrapped in a pun,
Finding truth in the jest—oh, what fun!

Adventures ahead with each friendly quip,
Join me for this zany, pun-filled trip.
For every stumble, there's a giggle in store,
A punning pathway opens every door!

Graceful Gags: A Tapestry of Life

In the tapestry woven of giggles and glee,
Every thread holds a joke, wait and see.
What did one wall say to the other?
I'll meet you at the corner, oh brother!

Colors bright like laughter abound,
A graceful dance in humor is found.
I saw a bee driving a car on a spree,
It was buzz-zy, indeed, as happy as can be!

Stitching together moments, no need for a glue,
The fabric of comedy—woven for you.
A playful reminder, amidst all the strife,
Is that gags can bring joy to the fabric of life.

So let us not fear the light-hearted jest,
For laughter weaves joy that truly is best.
In a world filled with chaos, a smile is a gift,
In graceful gags, our spirits will lift!

Whimsical Wisdom: Puns with Purpose

In the garden of knowledge, I plant my seeds,
Where wisdom grows, and laughter breeds.
I told a joke to a tree, it just stood tall,
It seems puns don't work on trees after all.

A fish tried to juggle, oh what a sight,
He flopped and he floundered, but it felt so right.
He said, "You can't scale this humor too far,"
As he swam away, I laughed at the star.

A worm in the apple, what life's tricky bite,
Said, "I may be low, but my humor's quite light."
In every crunch lies a hidden sweet,
With every joke, we make our lives complete.

So here's a toast to the pun and its cheer,
In laughter and giggles, we'll persevere.
Every mishap, a chance to grin wide,
In the garden of laughter, let's all take pride.

The Wit in every Woe

A hiccup of humor in every plight,
When life gives you lemons, just take a bite.
The toaster burned my toast, oh what a shame,
I guess it felt underdone in the game.

A cat that meows about lost fish dreams,
Says, "I'm just feline; life's never as it seems!"
With every scratch, there's a purr to be found,
In the chaos of woes, pure joy can abound.

A clock that ticks backward, such clever design,
Said, "I'm not running late, I'm just ahead of time."
So dance with the minutes, waltz through your fears,
In each tick and tock, find laughter through tears.

Let's juggle our troubles, don't drop the fun,
For in every woe, there's joy to be spun.
A chuckle, a giggle, we'll rise and we'll glow,
In the theater of life, let your laughter flow.

Jesting with Intent: A Poetic Exploration

I once met a chicken, her name was Sue,
She told me a riddle that was quite askew.
"Why did I cross? To get to the pun!"
And in that moment, my laughter had begun.

A pun-loving snail, on a quest for a race,
Said, "I'm not slow; I'm just keeping my pace!"
With each little joke, he crawled toward the line,
Showing all the world how he'd truly shine.

A burger and fries had a spat one night,
"You're getting too salty, you're never polite!"
Yet laughter ensued as they danced on the grill,
In every good jest, find the joy and the thrill.

So jest with intent, let your humor flow,
Like rivers of laughter, let your spirit glow.
For in every chuckle, there's wisdom held tight,
In the comedic light, we find our true might.

A Playful Path to Understanding

A playful penguin fell flat on the ice,
"Can't take this too seriously, just roll the dice!"
With a slip and a slide, he danced 'round his fall,
In laughter, he found he could conquer it all.

A wise old fox with a grin so wide,
Said, "Dear friends, don't let worries reside!"
With every word that slipped from his tongue,
A pun birthed a joy that was forever young.

The clouds played peekaboo with the sun at noon,
"Chasing rays is fun, let's dance to a tune!"
In the whimsical game of shadow and light,
We discover our truths in a world oh so bright.

So take a chance, let your worries unwind,
In the playful path, true clarity's blind.
Every giggle, a step toward the bright and the clear,
In a landscape of laughter, embrace every cheer.

The Irony of Insight

In a world where wisdom reigns,
I tripped over my own bad puns.
Each fall a lesson, rough yet sweet,
Life laughs with glee, and so it runs.

The irony lies in every slip,
A punchline waiting to be told.
I picked myself up, cracked a smile,
Turns out the truth was never bold.

With every twist and every turn,
I chuckle at the paths I take.
No straight lines here, just curves of fun,
For wisdom's catch has yet to break.

So here I stand, a jester's heart,
Wit emboldened by my blunders.
In laughter's grace, I play my part,
Each joke the light that brightly thunders.

Laughing Through Lessons

When life throws lemons, make a pie,
Then share a slice, and watch them sigh.
With laughter as my guiding star,
I learn that joy is never far.

A pun a day keeps worry at bay,
I stumble, yet I find my play.
In each misstep, a spark ignites,
A joke carved out from foolish bites.

As tickles dance upon my tongue,
I gather wisdom as I've sung.
With every giggle, insight flows,
And laughter's art forever grows.

So gather round, let's jest and cheer,
For life's a show when laughs are near.
No lesson lost in goofy wit,
In every pun, I find my grit.

The Paradox of Playfulness

In playful antics, wisdom hides,
Like kids on swings, oh how they glide.
Each giggle shared, a serious note,
In irony's hand, we learn to float.

The paradox dances in each jest,
With silly shades, we are laid to rest.
A clownish frown, a joyful breeze,
A foolish heart knows how to tease.

In whimsy's lap, I find my peace,
A riddle wrapped in laughter's fleece.
Each pun I toss, like bread to ducks,
Brings lessons sweet, not bound by luck.

So let us play, and never cease,
For in this game, we find release.
The serious world can take a break,
In chuckles' warmth, true wisdom wakes.

Proverbial Puns

A stitch in time saves nine, they say,
But laughter threads a brighter way.
In puns we find some wisdom curled,
Like pearls of joy in a hard-pressed world.

A penny saved is quite a tease,
When humor's found in every breeze.
So take a laugh, don't walk the line,
For giggles mark the grand design.

You catch more flies with honey's charm,
But joy's a net with equal calm.
In every jest, a truth is spun,
With laughter's echo, we all have fun.

So here's the punchline, ever keen,
Life loves a good and hearty scene.
With every quip, we find the keys,
To open doors of light and ease.

A Play on Words

A book fell on my head,
I only have my shelf to blame.
But can a shelf really hold me?
It seems I'm still a wee bit lame.

I told my friend to act natural,
He said, "I'm just too good at it!"
We laughed until we hurt too much,
Turns out he's just a little wit.

When a clock is hungry, it goes back,
For seconds it will always seek.
Time flies when you're having fun,
But puns are what make it peak.

I wondered why the baseball kept getting bigger,
Then it hit me, oh how profound!
It's all about the catch you make,
Not the ones that hit the ground.

The Humor of Experience

I tried to catch fog, but I missed,
It turned out to be a mist opportunity.
But why do we chase the clouds so high?
To find sunshine is our own community.

Never trust an atom, they say,
They're always splitting or exploding.
But I guess that's just their nature,
To keep everything in loading.

I asked the librarian for a book,
About paranoia, she whispered, "They're right behind you!"
Guess we're all just looking for answers,
Though some of them can smell the new.

I told my computer I needed a break,
Now it won't stop sending me chips.
Perhaps it has a sense of humor,
Or just really likes my flips.

Punderful Paths

I took a job at a bakery,
But I couldn't make enough dough.
So I rolled right out of there,
And found my bread on the go.

I decided to work at a farm,
Growing peppers was my fate.
But they said I was too corny,
Guess I just couldn't cultivate.

I named my dog Five Miles,
So I can say I walk Five Miles every day.
But now he barks at every distance,
Oh what a pun-derful play!

I had a fear of hurdles,
But I decided to leap with joy.
Now I jump over my own doubts,
That's the best trick the mind can employ.

Double Entendre Escapades

I'm reading a book on anti-gravity,
It's impossible to put down.
But isn't that quite the lift?
Just floating through with a crown.

The fisherman was feeling blue,
So I took him fishing on a whim.
But when I asked what he caught,
He said, 'Just a joke, not a fin.'

The bicycle couldn't stand up straight,
It was two-tired, what a sight!
But as I rode to balance life,
I realized that's just my plight.

I started a band with my couch,
But we couldn't find the right pitch.
Still, we jam on all the soft notes,
In comfort, we truly find the glitch.

Lessons in Laughter

When the clock is late, don't fret or fume,
Just say it's 'time' to make some room.
For every tick and every tock,
Find joy, it's not just ticking stock.

A bad haircut? Don't you pout,
Just flaunt it like you've got clout.
When life gets tangled, give it some flair,
A little snip can lead to a stare.

When you spill your drink right on the floor,
Just laugh it off, then grab some more.
For every slip, there's a chance to glide,
With humor, you'll take it all in stride.

In the grand circus of everyday jest,
Find the punchline, it's for the best.
So hamster on a wheel, keep moving around,
With smiles, you'll always be safe and sound.

The Wit of Wisdom

Why did the scarecrow win an award?
For being outstanding, not just adored!
In fields of gold, he took his stand,
A joke in the dirt, with a hearty hand.

To err is human, but to 'pear' is divine,
So slice up those chances, they're truly fine.
Lemons of life don't just make a drink,
Squeeze out the laughter, and never blink.

When you find a parking spot so rare,
Just say you're 'on a roll' without a care.
Even cluttered rooms can hold a surprise,
Just make room for quirks and laughs to rise.

Play on the words, let the humor flow,
For wit is a seed that continues to grow.
With every chuckle, blend joy and zest,
The heart knows best, let it jest and rest.

Puns and Circumstance

Why don't scientists trust atoms?
Because they make up everything, even phantom!
In the chaos of facts, let laughter arise,
A pun a day keeps the frowns goodbye.

In the bakery of life, don't be a loaf,
Raise your spirits, it's time to be bold.
Knead joy and laughter, roll it with flair,
A batch of smiles is beyond compare.

Where there's a will, there's a clever way,
If life gets sticky, just grab some play.
Like a joke on a string, pull it right tight,
Let's giggle together, from morn till night.

So celebrate puns in a grand parade,
With silly words, be never afraid.
Life's a comedy club, and you're the star,
So let your punchlines shine near and far.

Drill Down: A Punderful Journey

Setting out on a journey, all packed to the brim,
With puns as my guide, I'll never swim.
Through valleys of wit and mountains of cheer,
Each step a punchline that draws me near.

When life gives you carrots, don't just chomp,
Make bunnies laugh, give them a romp!
Spin tales of joy, let giggles unfurl,
In a world of jest, let your puns twirl.

If things get heavy, just lighten the load,
With laughter as wheels on this winding road.
Jokes are the fuel that keeps us alive,
In this circus of life, let the chuckles thrive.

So here's to the journey, let's punder and play,
With smiles as our compass, and puns lead the way.
Each moment's a giggle, let's never be shy,
For laughter's our treasure, let's aim for the sky!

Wit That Wakes: Smiles of Understanding

In the garden of jest, we plant our seeds,
Laughter blooms, fulfilling our needs.
A pun in the sun brightens the day,
Witty whispers chase the gloom away.

With wordplay's charm, we juggle with glee,
Each twist of a phrase sets our minds free.
We trip on the tongue, yet never we fall,
For humor unites us, empowering all.

A wink and a nod spark connections anew,
In the dance of words, we find something true.
So let's raise a glass to the fun we ignite,
In the world of the pun, everything seems right.

As giggles entwine, we bravely explore,
The lessons we learn leave us wanting more.
In laughter's embrace, we find our own way,
With wit as our guide, we brighten the day.

The Clever Curve of Learning

With every sharp joke, we curve around bends,
Each pun holds a truth that cleverly blends.
A twist in the tale teaches more than the tale,
In this ride of insights, we always prevail.

The key to the wisdom is hidden in jest,
Not just in the past but in smiles we invest.
When life deals a card, let's play with the line,
For laughter is timeless, and so is the rhyme.

In the classroom of joy, we scribble and laugh,
With each clever quip, we light up the path.
A lesson in humor, the brightest of lights,
Guiding our steps through the darkest of nights.

So next time you stumble, don't fear what's ahead,
Just say it with laughter, leave worries for dead.
In the clever exchange, we discover with glee,
The wisdom of puns sets our spirits free.

Meandering through Mirth and Meaning

On winding paths where giggles align,
We navigate wisdom one joke at a time.
A chuckle to guide us, a smile to steer,
In the maze of the mind, humor's always near.

Through riddles and jests, we wander with glee,
Each pun is a signpost directing you and me.
From the jesters of old to the memes of today,
The lessons keep flowing in a comical way.

In the tapestry woven from laughter and cheer,
We find hidden gems, truths crystal clear.
With each playful jab, our hearts come alive,
In the light of mirth, we learn how to thrive.

So let's frolic through life with puns lighting the night,
In the fun and the laughter, we always take flight.
With humor our compass, we'll never get lost,
In the journey of joy, we can't fear the cost.

Humor as a Teacher: A Poetic Reflection

In the classroom of smiles, the lessons unfold,
With a laugh and a pun, wisdom is sold.
A joke here, a jest there, they pave the way,
To truths that unite us, come what may.

In the punchline's embrace, understanding appears,
Went to school on the funny, left with no fears.
For humor, dear friends, serves as our guide,
In the quest for connection, we laugh side by side.

With quips as our textbooks and fun as the cost,
We learn from the moments we once thought were lost.
Through double entendres and wordplay divine,
Each chuckle we share becomes part of the line.

So here's to the wisdom that comedy brings,
In the laughter of life, let's spread our own wings.
For every pun told, there's a lesson within,
With humor our teacher, the fun's just begin.

Grappling with Giggles: A Lesson in Laughter

When you trip on your own shoelace,
Just pause and tie it with grace.
For every fall, there's a jest,
And laughter's simply the best.

If your cake flops like a fish,
Just call it an artistic wish.
Every mishap can be sweet,
With a slice of humor to eat.

When your phone seems to dance and ring,
Just declare it a new funky thing.
If it drops and hits the floor,
Put on a show, and ask for more!

So gather joy from every plight,
And laugh your way into the night.
A giggle here, a chuckle there,
Find the funny everywhere.

Smirks and Memories: A Comedic Chronicle

Never trust an atom, they say,
They make up everything, come what may.
A pun can brighten a dull day,
And help you giggle and sway.

If your toast burns with charm,
Just call it a crispy alarm.
In every failure there's wit,
Just laugh and choose to commit.

When your jokes fall flat as a tire,
Just fuel them with humor—never tire!
For every cringe, there's a smile,
Making the journey worthwhile.

So gather your quips and jest,
In this goofy life, be your best.
Embrace the smiles and playful glee,
For laughter's the key to be free.

The Wit Within the Woe

A cat walks decisively to a door,
But trips on its tail—not a chore!
With a twirl and a flip, it lands in style,
Teaching us to laugh all the while.

If you bake and your soufflé's flat,
Just say it's a pancake—imagine that!
In every flop, there's reason to cheer,
To see humor instead of sheer fear.

When a plan goes awry in a fray,
Call it a surprise, just for the play!
Every blunder, a chance to delight,
In the light of laughter, everything's bright.

So chuckle at woes, they'll pass by,
In the storm of life, just give humor a try.
A hearty laugh, a playful jest,
Is the kind of medicine that's truly best.

Satirical Strides: Lessons in Humor

When umbrellas flip in a gusty breeze,
Just grin and dance, do it with ease.
For a splash and a slide can become fun,
Making rain-soaked antics a true pun.

If you find a sock missing its mate,
Just whisper, 'It's gone on a date!'
In every pair that goes astray,
There's a tale waiting to play.

When your dog eats your homework again,
Claim it's a new breed of creatively zen.
In every mess and every scowl,
Find a spark and let it howl.

So step with a chuckle, leap with delight,
In the theater of life, take the spotlight.
With humor as your guiding star,
Savor the laughs wherever you are.

Chuckle Upwards: The Elevating Effects of Humor

A joke a day keeps gloom away,
Laughter lifts like a sunny ray.
When life gives you lemons, take a sip,
Add some sugar, let your spirit flip.

A pun retreats when serious strides,
But tickles hearts where humor hides.
In every chuckle, find insight rare,
Life's quirks dress us; they're beyond compare.

So juggle your worries, don't let them tease,
For smiles are magic, they aim to please.
A quick-witted quip can change your course,
With humor as fuel, embrace the force.

So keep it light, let your heart ascend,
With each punchline, find a friend.
In the comedy of our daily conundrums,
Humor may just give us better outcomes.

Anecdotes in Amusement: Lessons Learned

Knock, knock, who's there? It's wisdom's call,
Wrapped in laughter, hear its thrall.
When punchlines drop like surprise gifts,
They carry truths that give us lifts.

A friend once whispered, 'Don't be so tense,'
'Watch out for puns; they make great sense!'
In each mishap, there's joy to find,
It's all in the giggle, and the way we unwind.

Chasing shadows, with wit we play,
In the serious moments, don't dismay.
There's wisdom in folly, and glimmers in jest,
Let humor guide you; it's truly the best.

So gather your tales, all twisted and bright,
In the throes of laughter, find pure delight.
For every anecdote serves to remind,
That joy's in the journey, let your heart unwind.

The Punchline of Perspective

Why did the chicken cross the road, you ask?
To teach us humor's hidden task.
A simple jest can shift the view,
Give life's troubles a jiggle or two.

When woes come knocking, don't slam the door,
Instead, throw a pun and ask for more.
For laughter's lens can clear the skies,
And show the blessings in disguise.

So take a step back, let tension release,
In the comedy of life, find humor's peace.
A punchline delivered can soften the blow,
Wise-cracking truths help our spirits grow.

With giggles and gags, we'll march ahead,
With each witty jest, let laughter spread.
In every chuckle, a lesson equipped,
A framework of joy, where wisdom's skit.

Playful Parables of Growth

Once a tree learned to grow from the jest,
When squirrels teased, it stood with zest.
Its branches extended, reaching the sun,
With laughter and patience, growth's just begun.

A wise old owl hooted at fears,
Said laughter's the best way to dry your tears.
For when leaves fall, they make room for new,
In every loss, there's a chance to renew.

So dance like the leaves in a playful breeze,
Wit holds the power, if you just believe.
With every quip and a hearty laugh,
You'll grow tall in spirit, just follow your path.

Embrace the puns, let your heart play free,
In life's little dramas, find joy's decree.
For growth comes easy when laughter's your guide,
In the stories we share, let humor reside.

Lessons in Wordplay

A duck walked into a store, oh dear,
He quacked for some bread, it's quite clear.
The baker said, with a wink and a cheer,
"No bread for you, just puns for the year!"

A chef cooking fish said with a grin,
"You may scale it back, but don't let it thin!"
He flipped the whole dish with a twist and a spin,
"Now that's how you catch a good fin!"

Why did the scarecrow win an award?
For being outstanding in his field, not bored!
With crows all around, he just couldn't ignore,
"I just want to be fun, nothing more!"

The farmer told jokes, he couldn't resist,
"I'm egg-cited for breakfast, can't be missed!"
With humor so rich, you'd think he's a list,
Of yolks that bring laughter, a pun-demonium twist!

The Rhythm of Riddles

Why did the tomato turn so red?
It saw the salad dressing, that's what I said!
With leafy greens around, and fun to be fed,
It laughed till it blushed, 'Oh, me? I'm well-bred!'

What's a pirate's favorite letter, they say?
'Arrr!' you'd guess, but it's truly 'C' today.
Sailing through puns, in a jovial way,
He chuckled and nodded, "Let's seize the day!"

A bicycle can't stand up, that's a fact,
It's simply two-tired, with joy intact!
Pedaling through quips, we give it a whack,
"Keep rolling through puns," the laughter won't lack!

In riddles we dance, in humor we play,
Through puns and through jokes, we lighten the gray.
With each little chuckle, we keep gloom at bay,
Finding joy in the rhythm of words day by day!

From Puns to Profound

A wise man once said with a ponderous nod,
"Don't trust stairs, they're always up to something odd!"
He walked on past lunch to a mysterious pod,
That burst forth with laughter, oh what a façade!

A fish swims with friends, never alone,
But when they start chatting, it's a scale of its own!
They trade silly notions, 'til humor has flown,
And leave with a grin; they've grown from the bone!

The calendar laughed; it had days to spare,
Counting each moment, it sighed in despair.
"A month without weekends, how cruel and unfair,
But I'll make it funny, if you care to share!"

In puns we find wisdom, in laughter we teach,
The simplest of truths are the hardest to breach.
So let's gather our joy, let's giggle and screech,
From words to the core, there's a lesson to reach!

Irony in the Everyday

An umbrella opened in the sunny delight,
"Why's it out now?" asked the cat in mid-flight.
"I'm prepared for the rain that may strike at night!"
They laughed all the way, oh what a sight!

A fish out of water thought it was a joke,
"I'm swimming in circles while here's a fine poke!"
It splashed on dry land, as laughter awoke,
"Irony's funny, it's no hoax!" it spoke.

When toast lands buttered, we can't help but grin,
A flip in our fate, it's just how we spin!
"Who knew breakfast could cause such a din?
Next time, I'll land on my crust, not my skin!"

Through irony found in the mundane day-to-day,
We gather our chuckles, the funniest play.
From quirky to silly, we'll dance and we'll sway,
Finding gems in the routine, forever we'll stay!

Punny Reflections: Smiles and Sobering Thoughts

In the garden of thought, where ideas bloom,
A pun can light up even the gloomiest room.
A play on words, oh what a delight,
Turning frowns into smiles, making wrongs feel right.

Laughs are the sunshine in life's winding path,
Bringing joy to moments, dissolving the wrath.
Like a citrus twist in a glass of cold tea,
These puns, they refresh like a summer's spree.

Whispers of wisdom wrapped in a jest,
Sometimes the silliest lessons are the best.
A giggle can carry a heavy heart high,
With laughter as wings, we learn how to fly.

So cherish the puns, let them tickle your ear,
For hiding within them is much to endear.
In the maze of existence, let's follow the fun,
And toast to our mishaps with jokes on the run.

The Jest of It All: Wisdom in Witty Words

Why did the chicken cross? It's more than a chase,
It's a quest for the punchline, a dash of good grace.
Each quip a step closer, a journey we take,
For truth wears a mask of a giggle and shake.

With humor as our compass, we wander the absurd,
Finding nuggets of wisdom in each funny word.
So when life gets heavy, let's lighten the load,
For the jest of it all is a joyful road.

Like socks that don't match, yet they bring us such cheer,
Embrace all the quirks, for that's why we're here.
A smile is a ticket to places unknown,
Laughter unlocks doors to the truth that's our own.

So laugh until it hurts, and let puns be your guide,
In this chaotic journey, wear joy with pride.
For the jest of it all leads to laughter's embrace,
Wisdom awaits in each chuckle we chase.

Jocular Journeys: Finding Depth in Humor

Catch 22 in the comedy lane,
Where absurdity dances like drops in the rain.
A tickle of wit, a slapstick parade,
Where seriousness fades, and smiles are displayed.

In the race for the punchline, we often miss the key,
That laughter is treasure, a soft jubilee.
From puns about fish to jokes about bread,
We discover deep truths, while light-heartedly led.

Like a jester in court, who holds wisdom in jest,
The laughter we share can sometimes be best.
For while we may wander through shadows and gloom,
A chuckle can chase off the dark with a boom.

So let's prompt the giggles and bring forth the grins,
With puns as our lanterns, let the fun begin.
This jocular journey is the best kind of ride,
Where wisdom is hidden in humor's great tide.

Pundamental Truths: Life's Quirky Insights

A pun walks into a bar, ready to tease,
Whispering secrets like a gentle breeze.
Each word a riddle, a mystery spun,
Unraveling the truths as the laughter's begun.

There's wisdom in play, where lightness can dwell,
Like ringing a bell in a story we tell.
So don't forget joy, in this curious work,
For humor reflects what the heart likes to lurk.

In tales of the silly, we find something true,
Like questions without answers, in giggles we grew.
For the quirks and the oddities, oh how they shine,
In life's grand performance, they're genuinely fine.

So let's tip our hats to the puns that we make,
In this dance of delight, it's never a mistake.
For each joke is a glance at a truth we might miss,
Pundamental wisdom wrapped in laughter's sweet kiss.

www.ingramcontent.com/pod-product-compliance
Lightning Source LLC
Chambersburg PA
CBHW070750220426
43209CB00083B/240